Solutions for Creating the Learning Spaces Students Deserve

Making
Learning Flow

John Spencer

Solution Tree | Press

555 North Morton Street
Bloomington, IN 47404
800.733.6786 (toll free) / 812.336.7700
FAX: 812.336.7790

email: info@SolutionTree.com
SolutionTree.com

Visit **go.SolutionTree.com/instruction** to download the free reproducibles in this book.

Printed in the United States of America

20 19 18 17 16   1 2 3 4 5

Library of Congress Control Number: 2016956219

ISBN: 978-1-943874-18-7 (paperback)

Solution Tree
Jeffrey C. Jones, CEO
Edmund M. Ackerman, President

Solution Tree Press
President and Publisher: Douglas M. Rife
Editorial Director: Tonya Maddox Cupp
Managing Production Editor: Caroline Weiss
Senior Editor: Amy Rubenstein
Copy Chief: Sarah Payne-Mills
Copy Editor: Jessi Finn
Proofreader: Kendra Slayton
Text and Cover Designer: Laura Cox
Editorial Assistants: Jessi Finn and Kendra Slayton

Acknowledgments

I would like to acknowledge the work of William Ferriter, which constantly pushes my thinking and helps me improve as a writer.

Solution Tree Press would like to thank the following reviewers:

Rachel Amstutz
Principal
Bodkin Elementary School
Pasadena, Maryland

Eric Hardie
Principal
Carleton Place High School
Carleton Place, Ontario, Canada

Deborah Turner Ellis
Assistant Principal
Minnieville Elementary School
Woodbridge, Virginia

Julie Nickerson
Principal
Morse Street School
Freeport, Maine

Visit **go.SolutionTree.com/instruction**
to download the free reproducibles in this book.

Table of Contents

About the Author

 **John Spencer** is an assistant professor of educational technology at George Fox University just outside Portland, Oregon. Before this, he spent twelve years as a middle school teacher in the Cartwright School District in Phoenix, Arizona, where he used design thinking and creative processes for student coding projects, documentaries, and blogging. From 2008 to 2015, he coordinated and conducted frequent district- and site-level professional development on planning, development, implementation, and evaluation.

John is a frequent keynote and conference speaker, specializing in talks on technology, digital literacy, creative assessment, and project-based learning. In 2014, he shared his vision of the future of learning at the White House Future Ready Summit in Washington, DC. In 2015, he delivered the TEDx Talk *The Creative Power of Limitations*.

He is an active author, publishing both fiction and nonfiction. His research experience includes writing the chapter "Technology Criticism in the Classroom" in *The Nature of Technology*. He won Northern Arizona University's Educational Technology Graduate Award for his work in transforming professional development.

John holds a bachelor's degree in secondary education with an emphasis in history from Arizona State University and a master's degree in educational technology from Northern Arizona University.

To learn more about John's work, visit www.spencerauthor.com or follow @spencerideas on Twitter.

To book John Spencer for professional development, contact pd@SolutionTree.com.

Foreword

By William M. Ferriter

Can I ask you a tough question? How many students in your classrooms are truly satisfied with the learning spaces you have created for them? If your students reflect the national average, the answer is bound to be discouraging. Fewer than four in ten high schoolers report being engaged in their classes, and students often list boredom as the primary reason for dropping out of school (Busteed, 2013). Over 70 percent of students who don't graduate report having lost interest by ninth grade and, worse yet, the majority of dropouts are convinced that motivation is all that prevented them from earning a diploma (Azzam, 2007).

These numbers are troubling for anyone passionate about schools. They indicate systemic failure on the part of practitioners to inspire learners and warn us of the immediate need to transform education—a warning that school leadership expert and series contributor Scott McLeod (2014) issues:

> If we truly care about preparing kids for life and work success—
> we need *schools to be different*. If economic success increasingly
> means moving away from routine cognitive work, schools need to
> also move in that direction. If our analog, ink-on-paper information
> landscapes outside of school have been superseded by environ-
> ments that are digital and online and hyperconnected and mobile,
> our information landscapes inside of school also should reflect
> those shifts. If our students' extracurricular learning opportunities
> often are richer and deeper than what they experience in their
> formal educational settings, it is time for us to catch up.

Scott is right, isn't he? Our schools really do need to catch up if they are going to remain relevant in a world where learning is more important than schooling— and catching up can only start when we are willing to rethink everything. We need to push aside the current norms defining education—that teachers are to govern, direct, and evaluate student work; that mastering content detailed in predetermined curricula is the best indicator of student success; that assessment and remediation are more important than feedback and reflection; that the primary reason for investing in tools and technologies is to improve on existing practices. It's time to implement notions that better reflect the complexity of the world in which we live.

That is the origin of this series. It is my attempt to give a handful of the most progressive educators that I know a forum for detailing what they believe it will take to *make schools different*. Each book encourages readers to question their core beliefs about what meaningful teaching and learning look like in action. More important, each title provides readers with practical steps and strategies for reimagining their day-to-day practices. Here's your challenge: no matter how unconventional ideas may seem at first, and no matter how uncomfortable they make you feel, find a way to take action. There is no other way to create the learning spaces that your students deserve.

Introduction
What Is Flow?

It's a warm May afternoon, and my students have just sauntered in after lunch. They pick up their novels and individually sprawl out all over the classroom. I know, I know, students are supposed to sit up. Lying down and reading can lead to dreariness and lethargy. But that doesn't happen. Fifteen minutes into reading, the room is pin-drop silent. Nobody is falling asleep. Eyes stay glued to the pages. All students are technically in the room, but they all go off to various worlds. Some fight Voldemort. Others join Katniss in a fight against the Capitol. One student tears up over *The Fault in Our Stars*.

Ten more minutes roll by. Nobody says anything. Nobody looks up from a book. A group of screaming fourth graders passes our classroom, and still nothing happens. The room feels calm, but it has a buzzing intensity. The place feels electric. I glance at the students as they flip through pages faster and faster, dying to know what will happen next.

This goes on for an hour before I finally ask for their attention. Students groan.

"It's already been twenty minutes?" a girl asks.

"It's been an hour," I point out.

"No way," she says, shaking her head.

I point to the clock.

"I swear that we were only reading for, like, ten minutes," she argues.

"You think the clock is lying?" I ask with a smile.

"Maybe," she shoots back.

Fast-forward an hour. Frantic movement and intense discussions have replaced the quiet hum of reading as they design cardboard arcade games. This activity is louder, more cooperative, and more outwardly creative than the silent reading. Students tear off duct tape with their teeth (despite warnings to use scissors) and bend cardboard as they get closer and closer to having a makeshift pinball machine or Skee-Ball game. But despite the noise and chaos, the students' eyes have the same intense look that they had during silent reading. They stay locked into learning.

The truth is this learning experience rarely occurs. It's one of those little gifts teachers get, and it's hard to replicate on a daily basis. Yet we've all experienced moments like this before, where every student seems in the zone. Time seems to simultaneously slow down and speed up all at once. The class has a sense of challenge and urgency but also a sense of relaxation. You can intuitively feel something is different. The class is fully engaged. Students get lost in the task at hand, and they have no desire to walk away. The class feels different because student engagement is happening on a whole new level.

It turns out this type of in-the-zone engagement has a name: *flow*. When an athlete seems focused and dialed in, she is experiencing flow. When an artist gets lost in his craft, he is in a state of flow. Mihaly Csikszentmihalyi (2002), the theorist who coined the term, describes flow this way:

> The flow experience is when a person is completely involved in what he or she is doing, when the concentration is very high, when the person knows moment by moment what the next steps should be, like if you are playing tennis, you know where you want the ball to go, if you are playing a musical instrument you know what notes you want to play, every millisecond, almost. And you get feedback to what you're doing. That is, if you're playing music, you can hear whether what you are trying to do is coming out right or in tennis you see where the ball goes and so on. So there's concentration, clear goals, feedback, there is the feeling that what you can do is more or less in balance with what needs to be done, that is, challenges and skills are pretty much in balance.

Csikszentmihalyi (1990) defines flow as a state of *optimal experience*. In other words, flow happens in the moments when someone is fully engaged, present, focused, and alert—he or she gets in the zone. He mentions the following seven components to create a state of flow.

1. **A challenging activity that requires skills:** These activities tend to be goal directed and bound by some type of constraint. So they might involve a difficult problem that one needs to solve, a muse that an artist searches for, or a set of rules that an athlete must follow. These constraints provide a sense of challenge that makes the task enjoyable. However, a mere challenge isn't enough. Flow is most likely to happen when the challenge level matches the perceived skill level. If the challenge is too high, people grow anxious and give up. If the challenge is too low, people grow bored. So balance is critical.

2. **The merging of action and awareness:** When people experience flow, they often have a sense of losing themselves. As

Csikszentmihalyi (1990) describes, "They often stop being aware of themselves as separate from the actions they are performing" (p. 53). They feel a sense of command over what they do. The merging of action and awareness can feel effortless. However, the situation is often inherently challenging.

3. **Clear goals and frequent feedback:** When experiencing a state of flow, people have a clear picture in their mind of what they want to accomplish, and frequent feedback determines next steps. In any work, people must always have a mental picture of their goals and a sense of progress toward those goals. The feedback can be objective or subjective, internal or external, or physical or mental. Regardless, a sense of progress is a critical part of engaging in flow.

4. **Concentration on the task at hand:** Flow is not simply concentration. It's actually a hyperfocus on the now. It goes beyond simply staying present in the moment. When someone experiences flow, he or she has the ability to tune out anything that doesn't matter and focus on the critical elements of what matters.

5. **The paradox of control:** When experiencing flow, people feel in command of their situations. However, often people can't control these types of situations. For example, during a game, an athlete might feel in control, but the game's outcome remains totally up in the air. This sense of feeling in control but also working in uncertainty makes a task more engaging. While the work challenges the person and the task daunts him or her, flow makes the situation feel effortless in the moment.

6. **The loss of self-consciousness:** With flow, people feel like part of something bigger. They get so lost in a book or a work of art that they stop thinking about themselves.

7. **The transformation of time:** During flow, people lose all sense of time. Sometimes, a conversation with a friend is so engaging that hours go by but it only feels like minutes. Or someone may work on creating something all day and realize in the evening he forgot to eat lunch. Distortion of time is a critical element of flow.

Don't these components describe what we want in our classrooms—fully engaged students? Don't we want students to get lost and so engaged in what they do that they never look at the clock? Don't we want them to work with a sense of command and self-direction? Don't we want them to get fully motivated? Don't we want them to become passionate, creative, and empowered learners both inside and outside of school? But how do we pull it off? How do we make this happen?

Sometimes, it helps to look at examples outside of school. One of the most famous examples of flow in action occurred in one of the most legendary performances in sports history.

Flow in Action

I remember watching the first game of the 1992 NBA Finals between Portland and Chicago. The Trail Blazers dominated early by hitting seven straight field goals. The Bulls lagged behind, lost and unfocused. The typically dominant Michael Jordan trailed behind on defense and struggled to get the ball to the hoop on offense. Nothing worked. He looked shaken and nervous—hardly the larger-than-life legend we had grown accustomed to seeing.

Finally, Bulls head coach Phil Jackson called a time-out. Instead of screaming at and berating his players, he asked them to calm down. He talked about getting into a rhythm. They didn't change the strategy. They didn't get psyched up. However, even as a kid, I could see the change in Jordan's face. He looked calm and confident. He was entering the zone. You could see it in his eyes. Something had changed.

Then, it happened. Jordan flew around the court stealing passes, dishing out assists, and hitting every jump shot. The Trail Blazers double-teamed him, but even when they fouled him, he'd hit the shots and make the free throws. In one ten-minute stretch, the typically short-range-shooting Jordan hit six straight three-pointers. It was a classic case of an athlete hitting a state of flow.

Those moments of peak flow are admittedly rare. Michael Jordan wouldn't replicate a six-three-pointer evening ever again. A pitcher who throws a no-hitter probably won't repeat it on the next outing. An artist will have many days of feeling uninspired.

Even when it's not over-the-top impressive, many high performers can regularly maintain a state of flow. Serena Williams might not win a tennis Grand Slam every year, but she can get into a state of flow that regularly propels her performances. Neil Gaiman might not write perfectly every time he picks up a pencil and paper. However, he can hit a general state of flow that allows him to be a prolific writer.

This experience transcends disciplines. In a state of flow, a person's body just seems to do exactly what his or her mind wants it to do. Things feel effortless. Everything just clicks. It feels otherworldly. It happens with authors who can spend hours crafting a world in their head. You see this with coders, engineers, chefs, and accountants (yes, there are actually people who love numbers enough to hit a state of flow while solving complex financial problems).

So why not in our classrooms? Why don't we craft environments where students feel more focused, energized, and alive on the learning journey? Why does reaching a state of peak flow seem to occur only by happenstance, rather than through planning?

We want to see students get locked into learning in the same way a Broadway singer locks into a live performance or a chess master zones in on the game. We want to see students solve complex problems without zoning out or quitting in frustration.

Flow in the Classroom

Ask a student to describe a time when he or she felt in the zone, and chances are the answer will involve an activity outside of school. It might involve fixing a car, playing a video game, or reading a book. It might involve a deep conversation with friends, an art project, or a video that a student filmed for fun. What you won't hear is, "In the middle of that mathematics packet" or "When I was answering those reading comprehension questions to prep for the test."

Most flow experiences occur outside the school setting. This is due, in large part, to the industrial model of schooling. The designers of our factory-style education system didn't think about engagement. Horace Mann first introduced the industrial school model with the goal of unifying school into a common experience (as cited in Rose, 2012). Borrowing from the German system, he pushed for grade levels, common curriculum, and standardized procedures. Students were supposed to fit the system rather than the system fitting the students.

As Joel Rose (2012) describes it:

> The factory line was simply the most efficient way to scale production in general, and the analog factory-model classroom was the most sensible way to rapidly scale a system of schools. Factories weren't designed to support personalization. Neither were schools.

As the system evolved, schools valued compliant factory workers who could follow directions. They employed a system of punishments and rewards that ignored the intrinsic drive to solve problems, make things, and fully engage with the content.

The factories no longer remain, but the system does and, with it, the legacy of student disengagement. In fact, it's getting worse. Student engagement has been dropping steadily starting in fifth grade, before bottoming out at just over 30 percent midway through high school. See table I.1 (page 6).

Table I.1: Percentage of Students Engaged in School by Grade

Grade	Percentage
Fifth	75 percent
Sixth	67 percent
Seventh	55 percent
Eighth	45 percent
Ninth	41 percent
Tenth	33 perecent
Eleventh	32 percent
Twelfth	34 percent

Source: McLeod, 2016.

Educational institutions often respond to disengagement by focusing on skills interventions and making the content easier to understand—with the assumption that students disengage because they struggle with the content. However, that gives an incomplete picture. Often, the low achievement stems from low engagement. Disengaged students fall behind, growing more frustrated, less motivated, and less engaged in an ongoing instruction cycle. Boredom, frustration, and anger can lead to deeper behavioral issues over time (Stanney & Hale, 2012).

But not just struggling students disengage. We often see high achievers as students who get things done, who self-regulate their work habits, and who have a firm understanding of the material. Yet many high achievers aren't fully engaged. They do what they are supposed to do but nothing more (Schlechty, 2011).

We can do better.

About This Book

It's time to reimagine student engagement to go beyond compliance. It's time to rethink the current, most prevalent student engagement strategies. Often, the very structures we have set up to increase student engagement act as barriers to flow. Sometimes, even our helpfulness as educators disrupts the process.

Flow theory provides a lens that can complement our thoughts on behavior management and pedagogy. Flow starts with student buy-in and intrinsic motivation. It includes thinking about areas that we often neglect in the classroom. In this book, you'll learn how to help students reach a state of flow every day in the classroom.

Chapter 1 is all about motivation. You'll discover how to tap into students' intrinsic motivation instead of using extrinsic rewards as motivation. In chapter 2, you'll learn how to personalize instruction to match students' perceived skills with equivalent learning challenges to empower them as learners. Chapter 3 offers suggestions for shifting classroom pacing and moving from action to suspense to encourage meaningful conflict and growth. Lastly, in chapter 4, we'll analyze feedback and the importance of shifting from top-down to horizontal assessment.

The goal of this book is to demystify the learning experience to recreate the conditions that regularly foster a general state of flow. In other words, when you reimagine student engagement, it's less about dreaming of something new and more about making sense of those amazing flow experiences you've seen in the classroom.

When students fully engage in the learning process, they'll become the naturally curious, critical-thinking, creative people we want them to be. They'll view learning as inherently fun, which is ultimately what we all strive for: students who love learning. They'll take the desire to think, create, and question outside the classroom and into their world. That's what we want as educators.

Chapter 1

Motivation: Shifting From Extrinsic to Intrinsic Rewards

Think of the last time you reached a state of flow. Maybe you were creating something, designing a unit plan, inventing a recipe, writing a novel, or editing a video. Perhaps you got lost in a book and the hours flew by. Your state of flow may have come from running, hiking, or pushing yourself to the extreme athletically. Whatever you were doing, most likely you felt intrinsically motivated. You *wanted* to engage in this activity. The key factor might have been the challenge, enjoyment, or meaning of the task. But whatever caused it, this drive came from *within*.

Mihaly Csikszentmihalyi (2002) describes it this way:

> Flow is a type of intrinsic motivation, that is, there you do what you're doing primarily because you like what you're doing. If you learn only for external, extrinsic reasons, you will probably forget it as soon as you are no longer forced to remember what you want to do. Nor will you be motivated to learn for its own sake. Whereas if you are intrinsically motivated, you're going to keep learning as you move up and so you are in this lifelong learning mode, which would be the ideal.

In order to fully engage in a task, people must have an internal desire to do it. When a sense of personal fulfillment motivates people, they will likely take on challenging tasks without giving up. They are more likely to continue with a task because it is inherently meaningful to approach things with a growth mindset. Those with a growth mindset believe intelligence can change and develop over time. Alternatively, people with a fixed mindset believe intelligence is permanent—you either have it or you don't (Dweck, 2008).

Intrinsic motivation isn't a new concept in education. Behavioral theorists have long pointed out that intrinsic motivation can increase student engagement. For example, Edward Deci's groundbreaking 1971 experiment demonstrated how rewards actually decreased the desire to solve puzzles (Deci, 1971). Authors like Daniel Pink (2009) and Alfie Kohn (1993) have also shared the ideas of intrinsic motivation.

However, while intrinsic motivation is the starting point for flow, schools and classrooms often run on a compliance-driven, extrinsic motivational framework. That was the case for me when I first began teaching.

Learning From the Spencer Store

When I set up my classroom as a first-year teacher, I created a daily game system where students would compete *Jeopardy!*-style for intellectual dominance. The winning groups received candy bars. I later created the Spencer Store, with photocopied fake money bearing my face and a dollar amount. Every time a student turned in an assignment, he or she would get a specific wage to use Friday at the Spencer Store to buy candy or other small items. I admittedly had odd business hours, but I had the only shop in town, so I could pull it off quite easily.

It worked for two weeks. Then, students started complaining that the game wasn't fun and that the candy bars weren't enough. The students were right. Fun-size candy bars? Two bites, and they were gone. Where was the fun in that? So I upped the ante a little. I moved to full-size bars and eventually king-size candy bars.

That worked for another week. However, we soon had an inflation problem. I found that students initially worked hard, but then effort declined. Their motivation dissipated, not unlike the sugar rush they experienced after they ate the candy bars I had given away. I had to create better prizes and hand out Spencer Cash more often. I scoured the dollar store for better prizes, but three weeks into it, I could sense that it didn't work anymore. And on a teacher's salary, I knew I couldn't sustain it.

Unfortunately, we ran into deeper issues. A few students went rogue, engaging in covert counterfeiting operations and trading educational services for Spencer Cash. Top students began copying one another's work and then asking for bonus assignments to earn more Spencer Cash. Meanwhile, when we would engage in a previously fun classroom activity, students would ask, "Are we getting paid for this?"

On one occasion, during a Socratic seminar (a formal discussion based on a text), a student asked, "How much money will we get per answer?"

I stood there speechless, but he continued. "I have a long answer to give, but I can cut it down into a bunch of answers and make more Spencer Cash."

This struck me as in sharp contrast to the methods of Socrates, who never paid his students to answer questions.

The truth is my system hadn't actually failed. I had treated learning like grueling work. The students, for their part, had become excellent consumers. They gamed the system so that they could do as little as possible for the biggest reward.

The Spencer Store lasted a month before it closed down. During the short-lived experiment, I never once saw a student hitting a state of flow. Even in the early phases, when student engagement appeared high, no students were in the zone.

This story is not a unique one. Educators from around the world have shared stories of failed extrinsic reward systems that resemble my experience. David Ginsburg (2013), in an *Education Week* piece, describes how his reward system was more damaging than the moments he yelled at his classroom. Pernille Ripp (2014) blogs about how she abandoned reading logs. Student buy-in decreases, and teachers get stuck adding higher and higher rewards, leading to frantic late-night store runs or elevated stress levels as students rebel against the system. When we reward, we teach students that learning is not valuable but instead something that we must sugarcoat for them to swallow it. We trade a love of learning for cheap plastic trinkets. In these moments, student engagement is as artificial as the pretend money that we pass out. This artificial system actively works against the natural state of flow we want to see students reach.

Avoiding Extrinsic Motivation

Initially, I viewed extrinsic motivation as a complement to intrinsic motivation. I figured that it couldn't hurt to add another layer of motivation. But the reward system wasn't simply a layer added on top as much as an opposite force pulling students away from intrinsic motivation. Extrinsic motivation works great in the short term but has lasting bad consequences in the long run (Deci, 1995; Elias, 2016). Think of it like candy. It will boost productivity momentarily, but in the long run, you'll hit a sugar crash and fall apart.

Consider all the rewards for reading. When students get pizza coupons, accelerated reader points, certificates, or badges, they begin to focus less on the reading and more on the external motivator. They internalize the message that reading is an inherently boring chore that requires a reward—or worse, that reading is a competition, complete with winners and losers.

We need students to think of reading as inherently fun. I have never met a kindergartner who says, "I won't learn to read until I get a prize." Reading is rewarding when it comes with no reward. However, when we add a prize, we actually reduce the desire to read for the sheer joy of reading.

Moreover, extrinsic motivation can lead to risk aversion (Kohn, 1993; Svinicki, 2016). Students who focus on winning the prize fail to take the necessary creative risks to grow as divergent thinkers. After all, compliance will lead to a reward while a creative risk might decrease the odds of earning a reward (whether this is the loss of a prize or a lower grade). So why bother being innovative? Why bother trying a new method? Why should students take risks when they know that if they simply follow the path set forth, they will accomplish all the tasks the teacher created?

No wonder companies embrace extrinsic reward systems. They keep workers in check. On the other hand, many of the most innovative corporations have embraced intrinsic motivation (D'Onfro, 2015; Juliani, 2013). Companies have adopted Google's idea of *20 percent time*—or time for employees to spend however they see fit to serve their employer—to play for the sake of play. They know that the best way to keep workers in a state of flow is not by rewarding the work but by making the work rewarding. They realize that by empowering their employees and tapping into intrinsic motivation, they actually increase engagement and productivity. Classroom teachers have embraced this idea through Genius Hour, where students work on independent, choice-driven projects that they then share with the class. The idea is simple: students spend 20 percent of their school day pursuing projects that fit into their passions and interests—that intrinsically motivate them. Genius Hour comes from the fact that certain schools allow students to spend one hour a day doing these independent projects instead of doing a traditional homeroom or study hall. However, classroom teachers can integrate Genius Hour by allowing students to spend one hour per week on Genius Hour projects (Juliani, 2013, 2016).

This is an important distinction for the classroom. We know that our jobs matter. We know that our actions can inspire learning. But we face a humbling reality in knowing that ultimately we can't make a student more motivated to learn. We can, however, create the conditions that lead to a state of flow by tapping into each student's intrinsic motivation.

Fortunately, we have a better option. As educators, we can craft our lessons around the notion of intrinsic motivation. Instead of relying on punishments and rewards, we create lessons that spark intrinsic motivation by allowing students to connect learning to their own interests, incorporating creativity and problem solving, and tapping into students' natural curiosity and wonder.

Connecting to Students' Interests

One of the best ways to intrinsically motivate students is to connect assignments to their interests. My classroom Geek Out Projects are an example. As a class, we first explore the idea that everybody geeks out about something, whether it's ballet, cards, skateboarding, travel, or something else. Students then generate a series of inquiry questions before engaging in in-depth research. Their sources might be online, in a book, or through a digital interaction with an expert in their field of interest. Finally, they create multimedia blogs, podcasts, and videos. So, one student might research roller coasters and develop a listicle blog post on the ten best roller coasters and a video on how roller coasters work, while another student might do a sports podcast and article on the World Cup.

When students begin with geeky interests, they are more likely to take creative risks. Because they are already experts on the topics, they can focus more of their attention on specific skills in research and multimedia content creation. They also get more excited about the task at hand because it taps into their passion.

So why the need for student interest in the classroom? After all, with how much we have to cover, do we really have the time to consider what students might want to explore? The short answer is yes; we have to. When students delve more deeply into a topic they care about, they can tap into their natural intrinsic motivation (Cordova & Lepper, 1996).

But again, what about the curriculum? What about the standards? I made it work with these issues by starting Geek Out Projects at the beginning of the school year, when many teachers focus solely on explicitly teaching classroom procedures. Don't get me wrong, we still practiced classroom procedures, but we did so within the context of the Geek Out Projects. In addition, I tied our student-interest projects to specific Common Core English language arts standards that we focused on during the semester (National Governors Association Center for Best Practices [NGA] & Council of Chief State School Officers [CCSSO], 2010). In this way, the Geek Out Projects functioned as an authentic preassessment as well as a project. Thus, a student might be exploring the history of skateboarding, but in the process, she also worked on key Common Core standards (such as W.6.6, W.6.7, W.6.8, W.6.9, RH.6–8.1, RH.6–8.2, RH.6–8.5, RH.6–8.7, RH.6–8.8, RI.6.2, RI.6.3; NGA & CCSSO, 2010). The entire short unit and the subsequent lesson plans integrated each of these standards into a meaningful, student-centered Geek Out Project.

In the process, students began the school year feeling that they had valid interests. They asked their own questions, pursued their own topics, and expressed their final work to an authentic audience. Student engagement skyrocketed! Greater engagement begins with tapping into student interests. Give students permission to pursue topics they find engaging, and then build a community that honors multiple interests.

As students get older, they grow more independent. They develop tastes, find their talents, and geek out on things they find fascinating. They grow more assertive about their learning outside of school. Yet schools tend to grow more rigid with fewer choices and less autonomy as students move into the more departmental approach of middle school and high school. No wonder, then, that so many older students hit a state of flow in athletics or the arts, which they tend to participate in based on their interests. Students cannot feel intrinsically motivated while also feeling disinterested. Yet, many students operate under what Phillip Schlechty (2011) calls *strategic compliance*. They have high attention but low commitment and simply comply with the system to get the grade necessary to move on.

We can move students beyond strategic compliance—toward engagement (high attention and high commitment)—by tapping into their interests (Schlechty, 2011). Here are a few ways to do just that.

- **Tap into student interests with a survey:** Nothing beats a beginning-of-the-year survey to find out more about students. This survey can cover topical interests, themes, questions, values, preferred learning strategies, and questions they would like to answer or problems they would like to solve. Encourage them to respond honestly, and stress that, in time, they will realize they can trust you. You can then use these interests and preferences to inform both the strategies and resources you choose for your lessons.

- **Get to know your students:** After greeting students in the morning, ask them a follow-up question to however they respond. So if they tell you that last night was good, ask them why.

- **Allow students to develop the lesson's essential questions and project ideas:** Start with your standards or your unit focus and ask, "What do you want to learn about?" or "What do you find interesting?" It can help to have students generate a set of inquiry questions that you can use to develop the project.

- **Create Genius Hour projects:** Students can choose their topics based on their interests. They can own the entire learning process, including the topics, questions, strategies, and finished product they create.

- **Let students choose the topics:** Many standards are topic neutral. This is especially true in mathematics and language arts, where the standards are skill focused and do not require a specific topic. As a result, topics that students choose can still apply to important standards. For example, Common Core Reading anchor standard one states, "Read closely to determine what the text says explicitly and to make logical inferences from it; cite specific textual evidence when writing or speaking to support conclusions drawn from the text" (NGA & CCSSO, 2010). Students can practice this close reading with any type of informational text on any given topic. When engaging in research, students can geek out about a topic, and then they could blog about the topic for an authentic audience. A mathematics problem about a topic of interest is no longer an equation to complete but rather a problem to solve within a real context that matters to a student.

Incorporating Creativity and Problem Solving

Makerspaces and STEM labs offer ways to increase student engagement (Hom, 2014; West-Puckett, 2013). Makerspaces provide a community experience for students to share resources and knowledge and work creatively on their own projects. With STEM labs, students explore science, technology, engineering, and mathematics projects. In these spaces, students often get in the zone, hitting a state of flow. This doesn't surprise flow theorists, who first began their research with artists and makers (Nakamura & Csikszentmihalyi, 2009). After all, when we think of people hitting a state of flow, they tend to engage in a creative act. Artists, authors, and designers often reach that state because there is something inherently motivating about the process of making (Nakamura & Csikszentmihalyi, 2009).

I love to ask my students, "What did you make today?" Unfortunately, there are too many days when they can't answer it. They can tell me what they learned and can share the work they did, but they can't point to a single creative act that they got to do from start to finish. Yet, when they can point to one, it's like magic. Their eyes light up as they share what they worked on.

Creativity not only requires a deeper level of buy-in and engagement than compliance does but also a deeper level of thought. In Bloom's taxonomy revised, creating is the deepest level of thought (Anderson & Krathwohl, 2001). Students constantly solve problems, figure things out, and determine what to do next in this level of thought.

Creativity shouldn't stay limited to makerspaces and STEM labs. Students in every content area at every grade level should think creatively on a daily basis. You can intrinsically integrate motivating, creative experiences into your classroom in the following ways.

- **Consider using design thinking:** With design thinking, students engage in inquiring, researching, ideating, prototyping, and revising before eventually launching to an audience. It's useful in the corporate world, civic and social spaces, and the arts. You can use it with any standards at any grade level, but it works best when students are focused on designing a specific product (whether that product is a physical work, a digital work, an event, or a service). As a framework, it provides the necessary structure to develop creative thinking by moving through each phase in the design cycle.

- **Engage students in creative thinking through divergent-thinking exercises:** Divergent thinking is a creative approach that involves generating many possible solutions, finding connections between seemingly unrelated ideas, and looking at things from new angles. A typical divergent-thinking exercise might involve taking five random objects and challenging student groups to find as many uses for them as possible.

- **Remember that all students deserve to do creative projects:** Don't relegate creative work to a culminating activity or an enrichment activity for those who finish early. Embed creativity into your content in the same way you would integrate reading, writing, or technology.

- **Share your own creative journey with your students:** Tell them about the creative work you do and the creative barriers you have faced. This normalizes the creative experience and helps students see a role model for creative work. For example, if you write novels and have experienced a creative block, you can share that experience with your class in order to build empathy with your students.

Note that students can hit a state of flow outside the creative experience. As Mihaly Csikszentmihalyi (2002) describes it, "Even the most routine tasks, like washing dishes, dressing, or mowing the lawn become more rewarding if we approach them with the care it would take to make a work of art." Silent reading isn't creative, but it can lead to flow. Socratic seminars aren't inherently creative, but these deep conversations can lead to flow-like states of student engagement. The idea is to provide plenty of opportunities for students to regularly hit states of flow.

Extrinsic motivation treats learning like a chore that requires an external reward, but intrinsic motivation treats learning as a reward in itself. When students view the task as inherently rewarding, they are more likely to move beyond strategic compliance and toward true engagement. This, in turn, allows students to enter a state of flow.

Action Steps

The following action steps can help you shift from extrinsic to intrinsic rewards.

- **Abandon the reward system:** This can pose challenges in environments that build behavioral rewards into the school system. However, you can at least choose to avoid using punishments and rewards with the actual learning process. Pay close attention to how your grading system promotes or prevents student choice or creative risk taking.

- **Make intrinsic motivation a key part of your lesson-planning process:** Scan your lessons and ask, "Which of my students would find this intrinsically motivating? Which ones wouldn't?"

- **Ask questions:** When students sit down to a one-on-one conference, you should ask questions related not only to their work but also to them. Every moment provides an opportunity to get to know a student better, and every answer teaches you one more thing that can intrinsically motivate him or her.

- **Share yourself:** While each teacher must find his or her own comfort level with sharing personal details, it is vital to share something. Students must see us as real people with lives, interests, and ideas to pursue outside the classroom to trust us. When we share aspects of our personal lives, we can find commonalities with our students. This is how I discovered that a student loved zombies as much as I did, which led to other conversations.

- **Care:** Care not because you have to but because you want to. Students can smell an insincere teacher from a mile away. Investing in students is a great way to garner their trust.

Chapter 2
Instruction: Shifting From Differentiation to Personalization

Imagine you get invited to play on the Golden State Warriors basketball team. It might sound like a dream come true. But if the opposing team stole the ball from you ten consecutive times, you would grow anxious, angry, and risk averse. You might even give up. Likewise, if Golden State Warriors player Stephen Curry joined a pickup game at the park, he would get bored by the lack of challenge. Similarly, a novice cook would grow anxious and frustrated in a professional four-star kitchen, and an elite chef would soon get bored reheating hamburgers at a fast-food joint. The same is true in a classroom. Often, teachers will teach to the middle. However, students with advanced content mastery get frustrated and bored, while students needing intervention get frustrated, and their engagement plummets.

Flow theory offers a model for this concept of challenge and perceived skill. In other words, when students engage in a task, the way they perceive their own skill level needs to align with the challenge level of the task. The experience fluctuation model, split into eight states, represents the impact of challenges on different perceived skill levels (Massimini, Csikszentmihalyi, & Carli, 1987). Table 2.1 (page 20) illustrates this model.

When a low-perceived skill meets low challenge, students often experience a state of apathy. Think of a dull mathematics packet that leads a student to believe he's a bad mathematics student. Chances are he will check out. By contrast, a low-challenge activity with a medium-to-high perceived skill level might lead to boredom or relaxation. This is why strong readers might choose an easy read and find

Table 2.1: Experience Fluctuation Model

	Skill Level			Challenge Level		
	Low	Medium	High	Low	Medium	High
Anxiety	X					X
Arousal		X				X
Flow			X			X
Worry	X				X	
Control			X		X	
Relaxation			X	X		
Boredom		X		X		
Apathy	X			X		

Source: Massimini et al., 1987.

it generally relaxing. However, a student with a lower reading level (or a lower self-concept as a reader) might not have the skill level to make the read easy, thus he views it with anxiety.

As tasks become more challenging, things change. The student at the lower end of perceived skill will feel worried and eventually anxious as tasks get more and more challenging. But those same tasks will lead to a state of arousal in someone with a midlevel-perceived skill. A lot of creative work happens in this place, where a slight increase in challenge will lead to frustration but a slight increase in perceived skill will lead to flow.

It's interesting to note that flow requires both a high-perceived skill level and a high challenge level. Someone will easily experience a sense of control with a medium challenge. At this point, the student will most likely engage in the task but won't necessarily hit the state of flow that leads to optimal performance.

As a classroom teacher, you may have difficulty ensuring that students experience a high challenge level and a high-perceived skill level. This is especially hard in a class of, say, thirty students with thirty different skill levels and all sorts of barriers to self-efficacy that a teacher may or may not know about. However, teachers can take certain strategic steps to create these conditions more often.

Defining Personalized Learning

Traditionally, schools have responded to the relationship between challenge and skill level by differentiating instruction. For example, a mathematics lesson might have four levels of problems, ranging from pre-emergent to advanced. A reading class might have leveled reading groups based on each text's grade level. But even when teachers differentiate instruction, they may not always get positive results.

- Finding the right levels for each student can pose challenges. Logistically, differentiated learning can be a nightmare.

- Every task requires multiple skills. A student who has low comprehension might have high fluency in reading. A student with low computation skills in mathematics might excel in problem solving.

- When students fully depend on the teacher for differentiation, they do not self-direct their learning.

As a teacher, you know that each student needs to engage in a task that meets his or her ability level. The tiered approach doesn't consider the various mixed skill levels within a classroom for any given task. In other words, students do not fit neatly into a multitiered system. However, specifically catering instruction to each student can feel even more daunting than the tiered approach. It is unreasonable to assume that a teacher can write 140 individual lesson plans per day.

But what if there's a different way? What if the teacher doesn't decide on the challenge levels? What if you empower students to own a task's challenge level? Think of the times when students reach a state of flow outside the classroom. There's a good chance they select the task's challenge level, and they have the power to decide what scaffolding to use and when to use it to reach their goal. Whether they read a self-selected novel for fun or test out a new skateboarding trick, they move naturally toward more and more challenging tasks. Outside of school, students move through different levels seamlessly because they have awareness of their progress. They know where they are going. They have a sense of agency.

This is the essence of true personalized learning. Sometimes, people use the term *personalized learning* to refer to individualized, adaptive learning. Here, students get individualized support in key areas as they progress, alone, through a set of digital worksheets. Unfortunately, this fails to tap into the need for cooperative learning, and often, the systems focus on students consuming content, rather than having them think creatively or critically. Moreover, this approach fails to empower students to own their learning.

True personalized learning is different. It empowers students to be self-directed by self-selecting the challenge level and the necessary supports. Table 2.2 (page 22) demonstrates the differences between differentiated instruction and personalized learning.

Table 2.2: Differentiated Instruction Versus Personalized Learning

Differentiated Instruction	Personalized Learning
Teachers select the instruction based on student skill levels.	Students select the challenge level based on their perceived ability.
Teachers group students by tiered ability groupings.	Students work interdependently with other students from multiple skill levels.
Teachers provide prescriptive scaffolds.	Students select which scaffolds they prefer based on the available options.
Students work on the same standards at the same time.	Students select specific standards and skills that require additional intervention.

This personalized approach requires students to become self-directed and self-aware. Chapter 4 (page 41) addresses self-awareness in regard to student feedback. If we want students to embrace challenges, we need to improve their perceived skill level. This is why self-efficacy is so important.

Harnessing Self-Efficacy

Albert Bandura (1995) describes *self-efficacy* as "the belief in one's capabilities to organize and execute the courses of action required to manage prospective situations" (p. 2). In other words, instead of just simply increasing student skills, teachers need to create situations where students begin to believe in their ability to master a specific skill.

A student with low self-efficacy tends to avoid risks and difficult tasks, convinced that he or she cannot solve those problems. A student with low self-efficacy might quit a task before starting it or might choose a ridiculously easy task and never take on anything more challenging. Often, self-efficacy gets confused with motivation. However, self-efficacy is different. A student might feel highly motivated to do a more challenging task, but low self-efficacy keeps this student from moving on to something more challenging.

Also, self-efficacy is not the same as self-concept or self-esteem. Self-concept involves a perception of one's identity, and self-esteem involves how one feels about his or her identity. Self-efficacy is more about one's beliefs and attitudes about accomplishing a task. It often varies from task to task.

Students increase their self-efficacy when they believe they can accomplish a task. Teachers can best increase this belief by empowering students to own the learning process. This makes student agency critical. If students feel in control of the learning process, they will feel in control of the results and thus internalize the notion that they can accomplish a difficult task. So students must feel empowered to own their learning. By infusing our curriculum with choice and student agency, we can help increase student self-efficacy and eventually boost student engagement. Following are ways to shift to personalized learning and, ultimately, increase students' self-efficacy.

Let Students Choose the Task

The experience fluctuation model only works when a student feels intrinsically driven to accomplish a task (an idea we explored in chapter 1, page 9). A student experiences boredom and apathy with a difficult text if he or she does not find the text meaningful. Similarly, a challenging mathematics problem will fail to engage a student who finds the particular task devoid of any authentic context. On the other hand, a student might hit a state of arousal with a vastly challenging task far above his or her skill level if he or she finds the task deeply meaningful. Thus, a student who has a hard time comprehending the language in the Constitution might remain deeply engaged in the reading because of the direct connection to the rights we experience as citizens.

This is why student choice is such a critical component of instruction. When students have the opportunity to determine the task, they will be more likely to push through the challenging aspects. This results in a built-in level of commitment that teacher-directed activities often lack.

As noted previously, Genius Hour is one way to instill the power of choice (Juliani, 2013). Students spend 20 percent of their school day pursuing projects that fit into their passions and interests. Over time during Genius Hour, they create something unique and share it with an audience of their choice. Some students work collaboratively. Others choose to embrace solitude. Regardless, student choice often leads to creative risk taking and self-selection of challenging tasks.

Student choice doesn't have to stay limited to Genius Hour. Teachers can incorporate choice into daily lesson plans. At first glance, this can seem challenging. After all, teachers have to work within the confines of their curriculum and specific school and district requirements. However, within these frameworks, teachers can often add elements of choice. For example, students can select what novel they will read. They can choose what mathematics problems they want to solve. They can focus on a particular stream or historiographical approach when studying a theme in history.

Let Students Set the Pace

As a kid, I loved to read. I would spend hours with a novel or a magazine. Often, I would find the newspaper spread out on our kitchen table in the morning and snag a section that interested me. I didn't think of reading as a matter of fiction or nonfiction. It didn't have to be problem or project based. It was simply a part of life. I enjoyed reading, whether I read about a story, an event, or a strange phenomenon in science. At our house, reading was like breathing. It wasn't an event. It wasn't an impressive feat. We simply did it. We read with reckless abandon. We got lost in fantastical settings or in challenging ideas.

With this in mind, you'd think I would have enjoyed reading at school. However, I often groaned the moment a teacher passed out a photocopied magazine article or asked us to turn to a chapter in our textbook. At home, I got to explore my own destination, enter my own world, and ask my own questions. I could go at my own pace. I got to explore endless possibilities. But at school, I became a passenger on a ride going to a destination that I didn't really care about. Not only that, but the ride moved slowly and got stuck in a school zone. The car stopped every few minutes just to see that we stayed buckled in.

The end result was that I rarely, if ever, hit a state of flow when reading at school. But at home, I often found myself lost in a new world, spending hours in a book, unaware of the passing time. It wasn't a matter of fast or slow. I sometimes moved quickly through a chapter, and I sometimes slowed down and savored the words or wrestled with an idea.

Flow will most likely occur when students determine the pace. For example, in a 2005 study, Kevin Rathunde and Mihaly Csikszentmihalyi find that students in a Montessori school experienced flow more often because students worked at their own pace with fewer interruptions (as cited in Suttie, 2012). When they can hit a natural rhythm, they can get in the zone and reach a place of peak concentration. Helping students hit their rhythm can pose challenges for teachers. After all, each student has his or her own needs, interests, and pacing. Sometimes, you simply have to move into a new activity. However, teachers can use certain strategies to adapt to each student's pace.

- **Provide intervention and enrichment opportunities:** These will allow students who have gotten behind to get support and who have moved on to figure out an extension. For example, if students are doing experiments in science, some students can move on and do inquiry-based experiments (similar to a science fair) prompted by their results while others who struggled with the initial experiment can repeat it with more structure.

- **Move to a project-based, design-centered framework:** In this framework, students spend more time working independently. For example, when my students created documentaries, each student worked at a different pace. Some students were researching facts while others were editing videos or adding graphics. When we used the workshop model in writing, students wrote blog posts at their own pace, with varying word counts and varying post counts.

- **Transition less frequently, and allow students to work on a specific task for a longer amount of time:** When students are reading independently, allow them to spend a full class period delving into an article or a book rather than chopping it up with several breaks.

- **Give less work, but make it more challenging:** When teachers give students fewer tasks but increase the level of difficulty, students will be more likely to wrestle with a challenge to find the solution. This leads to the self-paced, intense concentration indicative of flow. For example, a teacher might give four really hard mathematics problems rather than a packet of twenty-two.

It took me a few years to embrace the idea of students working at their own pace. I used to set timers in class and stick to rigid guidelines. I constantly ensured that students remained on task. But the more I allowed students to move at their own pace, the more I realized that students didn't take advantage of the freedom. Instead, they hit a general state of flow and actually became more productive in their work as they set their own pace. For more on pacing, see chapter 3 (page 31).

Let Students Choose the Approach

If we want students to believe they can solve complex problems, we must allow them to figure out their own methods for solving them. For example, choosing specific strategies for students to use as they read, such as a rigid system of close-reading symbols, might do more harm than good. Students will own the close-reading process when they get a chance to create their own annotation system instead.

When starting a mathematics lesson on linear equations, I gave specific directions for solving one.

"I want you to subtract five from both sides," I said. I then modeled it for my students, who took notes.

"OK, next you need to get the variable on one side. Subtract the $4x$ from both sides, and you'll end up with just $2x$."

Students copied what I wrote. They seemed engaged. They paid close attention to my directions. I had even color coded the vocabulary and added a rationale for why I did each step. Things seemed to go well on the surface. I had nailed the direct instruction.

However, as they moved into guided practice, I noticed students looking anxious. "Am I doing this the right way?" a student asked.

"No, you can't take away $5x$ at first. You have to take away the numbers and isolate the variable first. See?" a student said, pointing to the board.

As I walked around the room, I noticed that students seemed concerned. They felt nervous and scared. Many of them had internalized the idea that they could solve the equation only one set way, when, in fact, they probably could have solved it ten different ways. The students who solved the equation correctly had learned a few skills but had failed to increase their self-efficacy. They had just copied my process instead of discovering their own way of solving the problem.

That's when I changed the process. The next time students engaged in problem solving, I asked them to choose their own approach. Some drew pictures or charts. Others graphed out the equation. Still others used the traditional algorithm approach. Next, they compared and contrasted strategies with partners and small groups, sharing their thinking along the way. Their metacognition and conceptual understanding increased as well as their self-efficacy.

When students choose their own strategies, they internalize the idea that they are capable of solving the problems. Even when they choose a process that fails, students can articulate what works and what doesn't work.

A teacher can allow students to choose an approach in the following ways.

- Let students choose a particular strategy to use while they engage in a task. For reading, some students might focus on making inferences while others ask clarifying questions or analyze the logic of an argument. Encourage them to practice a strategy that they struggle with. In my class, students selected specific strategies based on the feedback from our weekly one-on-one conferences.

- When introducing a new strategy (like close reading), allow students to adapt the strategy to their own style, rather than having them follow precise directions. Often, students get so hung up on the "right" way that they fail to focus on the task itself.

It's important to note that many students will struggle with choosing their own approaches. Traditional schooling has socialized students to believe that they have to accomplish a specific task one right way. But when they develop their own approaches, they increase their self-efficacy, and as they grow more confident, they will likely take on greater challenges.

Let Students Choose the Challenge Level

Sometimes when tasks are more challenging for students, they experience more anxiety than arousal. If they are risk averse, or if they have a low perception of skills, a high challenge might lead to failure (Massimini et al., 1987). Here, students become convinced that they cannot accomplish the task and thus fail to accomplish it.

Sometimes, students have to experience success with smaller, easier tasks before they move on to greater challenges. When students choose easier tasks, they don't necessarily do so because of laziness. Often, moving on to a difficult task scares them because they don't want to get something wrong. This especially holds true for perfectionists. In some cases, they have a low sense of self-efficacy, and they don't have an accurate view of what they can accomplish (Hart, Gilner, Handal, & Gfeller, 1998). So what can teachers do when students self-select tasks that are too easy? We can help students monitor their own progress so that they articulate their true skill level. We can also encourage creative risk taking by incorporating standards-based, mastery-based grading. Rather than assigning points and averaging the final grade, teachers can examine the evidence of learning (using a variety of formative assessments) and provide specific feedback describing the level of mastery in each standard. Students can then articulate where they are in mastery (their level) in each standard as well as what they need to do in order to move to the next level. Mastery-based grading allows students to resubmit work until they have reached a higher level of mastery. Students are not penalized for low initial scores, because the earlier grades don't count toward a final grade. So, students view mistakes as a part of the process. When students realize that risk taking will not lead to lower grades, they will select more challenging tasks.

Despite all these efforts, students might still choose tasks that are too easy. Here's where nuance comes in. You have to believe in your students even when they don't believe in themselves. In these moments, you can encourage students to go for a challenging task. In my experience, with the right trust and the proper support, students in these situations will often perform at a higher level and thus increase in self-efficacy. They will then begin to self-select more challenging tasks and shift toward a state of flow.

Let Students Choose the Scaffolding

When I took the training wheels off my daughter's bike, she pedaled forward, and I held on to the handlebars and talked her through the process. For an hour, I continued to help her, though I moved from the handlebars to having my hand at the back of her seat. With each turn, I let go of her seat earlier and let her pedal forward, and she would eventually fall off her bike.

"When should I let go completely?" I thought.

Then, it struck me. She would let me know. Even at six years old, she could quite clearly say, "I can do this on my own."

This is similar to scaffolding in the classroom. Traditionally, we view scaffolding as a teacher-centered process. A teacher creates scaffolds, or supports, that help students. A teacher then adds the scaffolding to lessons, and students work within this scaffolding to reach a challenging task.

What if this is the wrong way to think about scaffolding? What if we viewed scaffolding as less of a top-down, permanent structure and more of a tool belt that students could use? This way, students could access tutorials, short instructional videos, graphic organizers, and language supports on their own. Instead of waiting for teachers to modify a particular task, students could feel empowered to select what supports they need.

Teachers can help students select their own scaffolding in the following ways.

- Create tutorial videos that students can access at any time to see directions when they need them, rather than sitting through direct instruction.

- Create scaffolding stations where students can go to access additional tutorials. Provide anchor charts where they can reference past material.

- Find a place in class to share available language supports, like sentence stems and clozes (see figures 2.1 and 2.2).

- Use checklists and self-evaluations to help students determine where they need additional scaffolding.

When students select scaffolding, they can not only articulate their areas of need but also identify specific strategies and resources to help them along the way. Instead of remaining helpless and dependent on the teacher, they become empowered to pick up the tools they need for success.

Comments as Questions

"Why did you _____?"

"What made you think of writing _____?"

"Have you considered _____?"

"Is it possible that _____?"

"Have you considered the possibility that _____?"

"I was wondering, why _____?"

Comments as Statements

Agree and Disagree

"I agree that _____ because _____."

"I disagree with your thought that _____ because _____."

Clarifying

"I was a little confused about _____. Please explain _____."

Adding Your Thoughts

"I really enjoyed _____ about your post." (*Add thoughts afterward.*)

"You mentioned that _____. This had me thinking _____."

"You bring up the problem _____. I think a solution might be _____."

Figure 2.1: Sample sentence stems.

*Visit **go.SolutionTree.com/instruction** for a free reproducible version of this figure.*

Blog Comments

Paragraph 1: Agree and Disagree

"I agree with _____, but I'm wondering if _____ is also true. I feel this way about _____, because _____. What do you think about that?"

Paragraph 2: Questioning and Adding Additional Thoughts

"I feel _____ about your thoughts on _____. What you said about _____ had me wondering about _____. Have you considered _____?"

Paragraph 3: Quoting the Post

"You mentioned, _____. I agree or disagree with this, because _____."

Paragraph 4: Adding Your Own Thoughts

"I agree with _____. I also think _____."

Figure 2.2: Sample cloze.

Visit go.SolutionTree.com/instruction for free a reproducible version of this figure.

Action Steps

The following action steps can help you shift from differentiation to personalization.

- **Pay close attention to boredom and anxiety:** This ensures instruction meets the right challenge level for students.

- **Let students choose the amount of scaffolding they need:** Create spaces where students can easily find the resources they need, including tutorials, language supports, and graphic organizers.

- **Create self-assessments that measure student self-efficacy:** These can be a mix of open-ended questions and more specific quantifiable surveys to understand students' attitudes toward learning.

Chapter 3
Pacing: Shifting From Action to Suspense

One of the most universal elements of flow is losing all sense of time (Csikszentmihalyi, 1990). When artists, athletes, programmers, or scientists get lost in their work, they can spend hours engaged in a task without realizing they skipped lunch or forgot to turn the light on when it became dark. Contrast this with school, where students often work for forty-five minutes at a time before moving on to a new subject with content that teachers quickly go through. The standard lesson plan consists of multiple tasks that take anywhere from five to fifteen minutes. Teachers often try to increase student engagement by speeding up the pace and packing the lesson with action. However, flow theory reminds us that deeper student engagement requires a shift from fast-paced action to slower suspense (Suttie, 2012).

Rethinking Engagement

When my oldest son was ten, he was at that awkward age where he is too old for cartoons and too young to realize that nobody ever really gets too old for cartoons. As we sat down as a family to watch *Toy Story 3*, my son complained ahead of time that the movie didn't have enough action. However, he hung around for the first few minutes. Then, he stayed for a few more. Ultimately, he watched the entire movie and pretended he had "allergies" at the very end when his eyes looked wet.

Like most Pixar movies, *Toy Story 3* is built on suspense rather than action. Viewers feel suspense when something is about to happen. They feel this when characters act proactively even with the odds stacked against them. That intense conflict draws viewers in during pauses in action. Intense dialogue, nagging questions, strange events, and insurmountable odds make it hard for you to put a suspenseful book down.

Suspenseful books and movies rely on an emotional core, great conflict, and a series of actions to create a pace that draws consumers in so they become entirely unaware of time. The same is true with great lesson plans. The best lessons begin with a question, conflict, or problem. This sense of confusion fuels the mystery. Moments of frustration and tension occur. Struggling and waiting involve a level of suspense. In these moments, students can hit a state of flow.

Hitting a state of flow requires a seismic shift in how we view student engagement. Instead of packing a class full of action and clarity, teachers must slow down, engage in meaningful conflict, and allow for deliberate confusion so that students will enter into a state of flow.

Slow Down

In my first few years of teaching, I thought student engagement required an action-packed classroom. I had a rule that no activity should go beyond fifteen minutes. I kept the transitions fast and packed the hour-long class period with activities. Students walked in and had five minutes for timed bell work. We discussed the bell work in a think-pair-share, allowing students to think independently and share their ideas with a classmate and then as a class for another five minutes. We then moved on to ten minutes of direct instruction, a ten-minute group assignment, and a fifteen-minute individual assignment and then back to a ten-minute group assignment.

The pace was frantic, but to an outside observer, students seemed engaged in the process. However, most of the engagement resulted from novelty and action rather than purpose. It's hard to complain about an activity when it only lasts ten minutes. When the class worked, I assumed it had to do with the fast pace. If a period went by quickly, I assumed our quick transitions caused that. When things dragged on, I assumed that it resulted from a pacing issue.

Over time, I realized that this frantic pace actually got in the way. Students never had the chance to focus in a leisurely, relaxed way. In my experience, it takes time for students to enter a state of flow. Often, they won't reach that state for at least ten minutes.

I often notice this phenomenon in language arts classes. Teachers break a specific task down with constant checks for understanding. When teachers add note-taking devices and sticky notes to a reading, students never attain reading fluency. They stop students in the middle of writing to make sure they stay on target. Many of us do a midlesson teaching point, where we interrupt students while they work to point something out or teach another small component. But if a workshop acts to submerge students in a literacy experience, why do we interrupt them? Why not instead wait until the end to teach the minilesson or give the reminder? These disruptions, designed to help ensure learning and prevent boredom, actually prevent students from hitting a natural state of flow (Gallagher, 2009).

Cal Newport (2016) refers to this idea as *deep work*. It means that to hit a state of flow, students need to get into a place of deeper, uninterrupted thought. It's the opposite of multitasking. Instead of breaking things up and moving quickly back and forth, people settle into a task for a longer period of time. They can relax and zone in on what they are doing without any distractions.

Typically, school isn't designed this way. The traditional lesson-plan model breaks class up into short blocks of time with quick transitions. The bell schedule often moves students into a new classroom every hour. The curriculum's frantic pace means teachers cover content quickly without students engaging in deep work or hitting a state of flow.

To assess your own disruption pattern, ask yourself:

- "How much uninterrupted time do my students receive on average within a class?"

- "How long does it typically take my students to settle in and reach a concentrated state?"

- "How often do my students work until the bell or another scheduled interruption?"

- "What can I do while students work to keep disruptions minimal?"

- "How much do students rely on me to guide their next steps?"

- "How much control do students have over the allotted time that we have for class?"

- "How quickly do I engage a student who seems to be unproductive or struggling?"

- "Do any interruptions get in the way of deep work?"

One way to combat such disruptions is through *layering*. Layering begins with the idea that a particular task can accomplish multiple goals at the same time. So a team-building activity can also act as a form of assessment and give students a chance to learn language skills. Writing a blog post might give students a chance to learn about digital citizenship while also learning writing skills and building community.

A fellow professor mentioned an activity she uses in class that involves layering (K. Buchanan, personal communication, February 12, 2016). She calls it *breakfast with a theorist*. Each student takes on the role of an education theorist. Over the course of a breakfast, the student talks about education and suggests various solutions for the future of education.

At first glance, it seems like a fluff assignment. But this activity proves effective. Students have to know the theorist's backstory to navigate small talk at the beginning. This becomes a foundational reminder that theory doesn't emerge in a social, cultural, or political vacuum. Students also have to know the theory inside and out to articulate and defend the nuances of their theorist's position. Meanwhile, they get a chance to pick apart various theories and make connections between ideas and influences. Students experience a paradigm shift in how they view theory. Instead of mocking it as just an idea, they realize that all pedagogy has a philosophical foundation. They see theory as immanently practical and interesting.

Someone walking into Buchanan's ninety-minute class might think that students do nothing more than chat over doughnuts and coffee during this activity. However, they build community, change paradigms, make connections, think about their practice, and learn educational theory. Moreover, they hit a state of flow. Students fully engage, taking on a theorist's role and arguing about the nature and purpose of education.

Buchanan's activity looks slow because it happens in layers. She doesn't take fifteen minutes to lecture on theory, forty minutes to have them analyze case studies, twenty minutes to go over their essays, and fifteen minutes to do a team-building activity.

Consider a mathematics lesson. Traditionally, a teacher would focus on one specific standard each day and create a corresponding objective. So one day might focus on skills practice, and another day might focus on a concept standard. The results feel rushed and chaotic. But with layering, a teacher uses multiple strategies and standards as layers on top of one another. So a lesson on graphing also includes the standards on comparing and contrasting strategies, the conceptual standards of linear relationships, and the practice of identifying an equation by looking at a graph. This, in turn, frees students up to work on fewer problems for a longer amount of time. Students then get the time to hit a state of flow. Because the teacher doesn't rush learning, students can wrestle with the problems for a longer amount of time without worrying about hitting a time limit. There's a relaxed sense of mental space that allows students to stay focused.

The goal of layering is to select every task students engage in as intentionally as possible by finding ways it can accomplish multiple objectives at the same time. Here are some examples of layering.

- **Blending formative assessment into a project:** Instead of teachers stopping a project to have students take a multiple-choice quiz, they make the assessment part of the learning. So, students self-reflect or do a quick think-pair-share just to clarify where they are in their learning. The teacher can assess by using observations or offering feedback in the moment.

- **Blending subjects:** For example, a social studies teacher integrates reading and writing, or an English teacher supports history or economics. This way, students connect specific texts to multiple subjects. Thus a mathematics lesson on relationships and functions can coincide with a lesson on variables in developing science experiments. A social studies blog could incorporate standards from reading and writing.

- **Embedding intervention and enrichment into differentiated instruction:** Students can practice a particular skill to improve or enrich during a high-interest learning activity. In other words, students can choose to practice a specific reading skill while they read an article of their choosing at their reading level.

- **Integrating technology into a lesson:** Refrain from stopping a lesson to do a specific technology lesson. Often, teachers will do a specific lesson on a technology skill before having students use that skill in a specific lesson. This can be a time waster; especially when certain students already have mastered the technology level or can learn the skills through experimentation. Instead of teaching students how to create videos, provide tutorials and tips on video composition and have students create their subject-specific videos while accessing technology help only when needed.

- **Finding standards that connect:** Students might spend a week researching a topic, and in the process, they can hit multiple reading standards.

The idea here is to view tasks as holistic and connective rather than singular and isolated. When you put this idea into action, students can spend the time they need working more slowly, more deliberately, until they hit a state of flow. To them, it feels like they are moving slower, and it might even look inefficient. But this pace actually works far more efficiently than the traditional pace of a lesson.

It can feel scary to slow things down. What if students stop paying attention? What if they get bored? What if they check out entirely? What if they finish early? However, in my experience, a slower pace actually allows students who need additional help to complete their tasks while those ahead of the curve can take their learning to a new level.

Suspense requires slowing down. The Department of Motor Vehicles might move slowly, but you experience the opposite of a state of flow when you go there, so time doesn't fly by. The possibility of boredom makes it important to engage students in meaningful conflict.

Engage in Meaningful Conflict

Think back to the *Toy Story 3* example. The story worked because of the conflict. The larger problem drove the suspense of the story. The same is true of great lesson plans. Think of conflict less as a negative issue between people (or *relational conflict*) and more as a problem to solve or a puzzle to complete. Again, students have to engage in work they find meaningful to have intrinsic motivation. This conflict might begin with a sense of wonder or curiosity. It could involve an intriguing, complicated problem in mathematics or a sense of inquiry in science. It might involve an essential question in social studies or an interesting argument in a language arts class. When students engage with meaningful conflict, it creates suspense. The class doesn't have to be packed with action. The pace might be slower, but students begin to hyperfocus and hit a state of flow.

Allow for Deliberate Confusion

Teachers can also tap into suspense by engaging in *deliberate confusion*—encouraging problem solving by withholding an answer or solution for a short time. This sounds counterintuitive and even paradoxical, but deliberate confusion can act as a powerful force for deeper learning and clarity of understanding. For example, in a study on science content, students watched two types of short videos (Muller, 2008). In the first set of videos, they learned in a straightforward, clear, systematic method. Although they rated themselves high on perceived knowledge attainment, they actually scored low when tested on the content later. By contrast, when they watched videos where the physical phenomena confused them and they had to write a hypothesis and see it confirmed or denied in the video, they learned the content at a deeper level and retained it longer (Muller, 2008). The confusing videos piqued student curiosity and naturally led to inquiry. At the end of the videos, students could see how their hypotheses were either confirmed or denied.

Students need confusion, conflict, and more time to wrestle with hard questions. When this happens, they mentally engage with the content and end up learning at a deeper level. Going back to flow theory, when students reach a state of optimal performance, they often deal with confusing and intriguing challenges. They solve complex problems—and even feel effortless doing it. They tap into the universal need for suspense rather than just action.

Annie Murphy Paul (2013) describes it this way:

> We short-circuit this process of subconscious learning, however, when we rush in too soon with an answer. It's better to allow that confused, confounded feeling to last a little longer—for two reasons. First, not knowing the single correct way to resolve a problem allows us to explore a wide variety of potential explanations, thereby giving us a deeper and broader sense of the issues involved. Second, the feeling of being confused, of not knowing what's up, creates a powerful drive to figure it out. We're motivated to look more deeply, search more vigorously for a solution, and in so doing we see and understand things we would not have, had we simply been handed the answer at the outset.

Reducing Distractions and Clutter

With a slower pace, friendly conflict, and deliberate confusion, students should naturally reach a state of flow. However, sometimes students still struggle to focus. If the classroom environment has too many distractions, they will struggle to get in the zone. A cluttered classroom is the physical equivalent to having too much action and transition in the lesson. However, when teachers reduce distractions, students can focus on the natural suspense that arises from engaging in a meaningful challenge.

In order to reduce distractions, simplify your space. Research studies (Fischer, Godwin, & Seltman, 2014) demonstrate that students will better engage in a less busy physical environment. Create a warm, welcoming environment. You don't need to strip your walls of all posters and turn the place into a bare, clinical environment. But many scaffolding devices can actually serve as distractions. Walls covered with helpful tools, such as anchor charts, word walls, and other visuals, create overstimulation. Students cannot see the resources that might actually support their learning; instead, they feel flooded with too much knowledge to take in. In our helpfulness, we therefore create mental clutter that students then need to use energy to drown out.

You can reduce distractions and clutter in the following nine ways.

1. **Get rid of the teacher's desk:** I've seen classrooms with a teacher's desk and table, minifridge, microwave, and coffeepot. At some point, they begin to feel less like classrooms and more like studio apartments. For teachers not ready to remove their desk altogether, think of its placement. Does it (and additional items) create clutter? Do you need it? Does it create a physical barrier between you and students? When you abandon the teacher's desk, you open up the classroom space and make it easier to move around. But it also reduces the physical barrier between teachers and students, thereby opening up the communication and making the teacher more approachable.

2. **Create one anchor chart that you can flip:** Rather than having multiple single-page anchor charts, use one chart that flips. Add tabs to the chart to make it more user friendly. Also, add anchor charts to a classroom website or blog so they become easy-to-access resources for students.

3. **Choose words for your word wall selectively:** Only add the most essential words that students may need to reference, and then cycle through words as needed. Know when students have mastered words or definitions, and provide students who still need a reference guide with a personal one-word guide. A personalized word guide might be a handout, flipchart, or shared digital document that teachers could share with specific students.

4. **Ditch the kidney-shaped table:** Meet in small groups with students at their current tables or desks. This reduces clutter while also allowing you to get closer to students.

5. **Allow for more movement within the classroom:** This seems counterintuitive, but when you allow students to move around, they can get into a state of flow. They can get comfortable and focus. Traditionally, schools have discouraged movement with the assumption that it leads to distractions. However, think of the last time you had to stay still in a meeting without getting to move. Chances are you had a hard time staying focused.

6. **Allow students to choose where they sit:** When students get to choose where they sit, whether at a desk or on the floor, and even whom they sit by, it immediately creates a different power balance in the classroom, allowing them to feel that they matter more. That deeper sense of belonging and trust will help them reach a state of flow. If a few students cannot handle the responsibility of choosing their own seats, then discuss seating accordingly with those few students. Do not punish a whole class for a few students' poor decisions.

7. **Create standing centers:** Some students focus better when they have the freedom to stand. You can create standing centers for them in simple ways; for example, take a heavy bookshelf, and pull it away from the wall diagonally. Let students stand by it while they work.

8. **Adapt the space to the task:** Flow looks different while reading a novel versus building a mock roller coaster. Silent reading might require students to sit individually, spreading out and staying still. By contrast, the mock roller coaster might have tons of movement with students standing in groups and making noise. These tasks require differentiated spaces so that flow can happen at both an individual and small-group level.

9. **Allow students to change spaces as they see fit:** When students know that they can adapt an environment to fit their needs, they will be more likely to commit to the task at hand. Some students might need to move or stand. Some might need to find quiet spaces where they can hit a state of flow more easily.

Sometimes, student engagement problems are less about external distractions and more about an internal focus issue. Certain students struggle with focusing on the task at hand. They feel anxious, bored, or restless. Often, they simply struggle to reach that place of deep work. Teachers can cultivate this focus through *mindfulness*—purposely paying attention to one's thoughts and feelings (Jennings, 2015).

For example, Lisa Noble, a language educator in Ontario, begins each class period with a mindfulness activity. She describes it this way: "Many students come into class with experiences that can make it hard to focus. Their only options are fight or flight. They don't have any real strategies for settling themselves" (personal communication, December 14, 2015).

She uses deep breathing, drawing, and extended-time activities so students can think, doodle, or engage in private meditation to allow for mindfulness. She notes:

> These might seem strange to certain people. They might even seem like a waste of time. However, it actually increases productivity. Students are more aware of where they are at and then they move into an activity with more focus and clarity. If I take the time to do the settling in, we get more accomplished. We are far more productive.

Students can also hit a state of group flow more easily. "My students are able to collaborate better after mindfulness. I'm not having to put out fires in each group," says Noble.

Noble advises teachers to start out slowly with mindfulness so that students can build up endurance in staying focused: "Figure out what works for you and, more importantly, what works for your students."

These small changes can help prevent external and internal distractions and allow students to hit a state of flow. Students experience a greater sense of suspense as they focus on a meaningful challenge rather than physical distractions. However, the biggest challenges in promoting flow often relate to instruction.

Adding More Thinking and Less Work

One of the best ways to allow students to reach a state of flow is to push for more thinking with less but more meaningful work. This doesn't mean students spend less time reading, writing, or working. Instead, they go more in depth for a longer amount of time with fewer interruptions. When this happens, they have that *Toy Story 3*–like feeling where they might experience less action (fewer tasks) but more suspense (deeper thinking in the core problems they are trying to solve, skills they are trying to master, or concepts they are trying to make sense of). In other words, they are thinking more but working less.

In mathematics, this might mean students spending more time wrestling with a few difficult problems rather than filling out a packet of them. It might involve them verbally explaining a process to one another rather than describing it in a written format. They might take extended time to figure out a process, rather than zipping through multiple problems in a direct-instruction-and-guided-practice cycle. The goal isn't practicing multiple problems so much as developing a rhythm and stamina as problem solvers and mathematicians.

In reading, this might mean ditching the note cards, graphic organizers, and sticky notes and instead simply reading. It might mean allowing students to figure out when they want to use a close-reading strategy and when they want to read without stopping. This way, they go in depth and hit a rhythm as readers, delving into the natural suspense that occurs when they are discovering new information or diving into a story.

This can feel challenging for teachers. So many structures are designed to help students. However, if the student doesn't need help, these scaffolding structures simply disrupt flow. Kelly Gallagher (2009) describes these practices as *readicide*. Here, the well-intentioned supports actually slow down learning and reduce student engagement. Gallagher (2010) describes an assignment where students left sticky notes on every page of *Romeo and Juliet*:

> As a result [of the notes], this timeless work became an extended worksheet. Its beauty—its value—got lost in a sea of sticky notes. Imagine going to see a great movie, only to have the projectionist stop the film every four minutes to see if you are taking notes. Now imagine being forced to read a novel this way, and you'll see how over-teaching destroys students' desire to read.

This natural sense of suspense often drives our flow experiences. Whether it is the challenge of tackling a new skill, the intrigue of discovering new information, or the conflict inherent in great problems, we are more likely to experience flow when suspense pulls us in. However, this type of suspense requires slower pacing, less action, and fewer interruptions. By reducing these distractions, teachers can create environments where students are able to experience suspense and reach a state of flow.

Action Steps

The following action steps can help you shift from action to suspense.

- **Layer instruction:** When planning lessons, think about tasks that can accomplish multiple goals at the same time. Find standards that connect to one another.

- **Use deep work:** Create lessons that allow students to delve deeper into a topic for a longer period of time.

- **Limit distractions:** Do whatever you can to limit both external and internal distractions, such as using mindfulness.

- **Go in depth longer:** Design learning experiences that require more thinking but less work.

Chapter 4

Feedback: Shifting From Top-Down to Horizontal Assessment

My oldest son got lost in the moment as he worked on a cardboard pinball machine. He studied his sketch, jotted down a few notes, measured a piece, and cut it out. When this didn't work, he shortened the piece and tested it out.

"What about rulers?" he mumbled to himself before going to his desk and pulling out two metal rulers to use as flippers.

I glanced at my daughter. She was creating a picture book about a ninja princess who had to stop robots from attacking a school. Like her brother, she made tiny tweaks to her design. Additionally, like her brother, she mumbled to herself about what she needed to add. I looked over to my middle son. He muttered to himself as well as he sketched a picture. Some families are super athletic or crazy artistic. Not us. We talk to ourselves. It's our thing.

Although my three kids engaged in different activities, they each experienced hyperfocus. They were in the zone, lost in their own worlds. In all three activities, they had a clear sense of progress. They had an awareness of feedback and constantly made adjustments as a result. In other words, they owned the assessment process. Instead of a top-down approach, they engaged in self-assessment. It was a horizontal, democratic version of assessment that didn't begin and end with an adult.

Consider a video game. Part of what allows people to hit a state of flow while playing one is that they go through a constant, incremental progression. Some of this involves the increasing level of challenge as the game progresses. However, a more constant element is the immediate feedback the player gets as he or she moves through the game. If a Goomba hits Mario, you, as a player, know that you failed, and as a result, you get the chance to try again to move on. As when you build a cardboard pinball machine or play a video game, you need an awareness of progress to hit a state of flow in the classroom.

Having an Awareness of Progress

In flow theory, both Jeanne Nakamura and Mihaly Csikszentmihalyi (2009) identify a fusion of action and awareness as one of the key components to hitting a state of flow. Owen Schaffer (2013) emphasizes this idea in his seven flow conditions for progress.

1. Knowing what to do

2. Knowing how to do it

3. Knowing how well you are doing

4. Knowing where to go (if navigation is involved)

5. Having high-perceived challenges

6. Having high-perceived skills

7. Having freedom from distractions

The first four conditions essentially relate to awareness of progress. Yet, oddly, people usually stay almost unaware of ongoing self-assessment as they experience a state of flow. Students monitor their performance and adjust, making slight variations to improve. They have a clear sense of how they are doing and where they are going. Still, they don't overthink. For example, a gymnast will not stop her routine and say, "Let me take a self-assessment, gather some feedback, and move on." Instead, the feedback seems to fuse with the action. However, what truly happens is that people stay so aware of their progress that it feels seamless. They have a goal in mind and a constant progression. The key is that they don't stop what they're doing to monitor progress. They monitor their progress constantly, incrementally, and instantaneously.

For this to happen in the classroom, students need to have what Csikszentmihalyi (1990) describes as "clear proximal goals and immediate feedback about the progress being made" (p. 54). This requires students to know their mastery of a skill or concept ahead of time. It also requires that students have a clear set of goals to visualize. It then requires that students not only receive immediate feedback but also stay fully aware of the feedback in comparison to their goals. But this sense of awareness isn't enough. Students must also have the ability to monitor their performance and adjust based on feedback. This constant cycle of feedback and adjustment often looks instantaneous.

This cycle can create challenges in the classroom. Sometimes, students struggle with defining goals. Other times, they lack the metacognitive skills to articulate where they are going and how they are doing. It helps if they assess their learning as they go.

Owning the Assessment Process

When I taught a reading intervention block as a middle school teacher, I noticed that students cringed at the word *assessment*. When I asked students to list words they associated with *assessment*, the most popular answers were *boring*, *scary*, *random*, and *slow*. Students viewed assessment as something they had to take rather than something they regularly engaged in. Perhaps this is because assessment has traditionally been teacher driven, judgmental, and removed from the learning process.

But what if we viewed assessment as part of the learning process? A student doesn't take an assessment. A student assesses, alongside a teacher, in a constant, ongoing conversation. Assessing happens when students understand where they are going and make adjustments based on feedback during a constant dialogue of checking for understanding.

When we treat assessment as something that students must take rather than something that they do, students view assessment as an artificial other, a dark place that, unlike their own work, forbids them from working collaboratively, making their own decisions, using technology, or using flexible thinking. When students can assess as they go, they will be more likely to have the time needed to reach a state of flow. They grow more self-aware and more confident in their ability to make adjustments based on the feedback they gather on their own.

It helps to think about a student-centered, rather than teacher-centered, approach to assessment: horizontal assessment (see table 4.1).

Table 4.1: Top-Down Versus Horizontal Assessment

Top-Down Assessment	Horizontal Assessment
It exists to inform the teacher.	It exists to inform students.
The teacher initiates it.	Students or the teacher initiate it.
It takes the form of a monologue.	It takes the form of a conversation.
The teacher assesses.	The teacher, students, and peers assess.
The goal is a score.	The goal is a sense of awareness of progress.
Learning stops for students to take an assessment.	Assessments occur throughout the learning process.
The teacher sets goals and monitors progress.	Students set goals and monitor progress with the teacher's guidance.

When students experience a horizontal approach to feedback and assessment, they feel empowered to own the assessment process. As a result, they get more engaged in the assessment process, with a deeper understanding of where they are going and what they need to do next (Smith, Rook, & Smith, 2007). These elements are vital for reaching a state of flow, and students can tap into these transferable thinking skills when they engage in meaningful work outside of school.

Top-level performers in any industry have a clear understanding of progress. They have the uncanny ability to monitor their performance and adjust as they go. We want this for our students, and teachers can implement specific strategies to allow students to increase their awareness and make the constant, necessary adjustments they must make to thrive. This requires a horizontal system of assessment where students are actively engaged in monitoring their own progress.

Self-Assessment

Students can grow in self-awareness through two ongoing forms of self-assessment: (1) *in-the-moment self-assessment* and (2) *after-the-fact self-assessment*.

Students who struggle with metacognition may have difficulty with in-the-moment self-assessment, but teachers can model the process during direct instruction. For example, a teacher might do a read-aloud and stop to say, "So where am I? What do I get? What part do I find tricky?" As they model the process, they can bring students into the conversation by asking, "What kinds of questions might I ask myself as I read? How do I know that I understand it right now?"

It can feel artificial when students first practice this type of self-assessment. Students who aren't used to pondering their thinking might struggle with engaging in an internal dialogue about progress. However, the more they practice it, the more likely they'll hit a place of automaticity. Slowly, it becomes a habit.

With after-the-fact self-assessment, students think through reflection questions and articulate how they have done. You might ask the following questions in your classroom.

- "How do you feel about your work? What adjectives would you use to describe your feelings toward your finished product?"
- "What would you improve if you had more time?"
- "What part of your work are you the most proud of?"
- "What did you learn along the way? Describe any new skills or concepts you acquired."
- "What did you learn about yourself based on this experience?"
- "What part was the hardest for you? Why?"
- "What part was the easiest for you? Why?"

- "Would you do something similar to this in your free time? Why or why not?"
- "How could you build on this assignment or project in the future?"
- "What are your next steps?"

In terms of timing, the questions work well as a warm-up activity, a midlesson break, or an exit slip. I've had some great success using Google Forms (www.google .com/forms) as a survey tool for this type of self-reflection. You can also add quantitative elements (such as "Rate how you did on a scale of 1 to 10"). Then, using Google Forms, you can look at general class trends. Although reflection questions are powerful ways to inspire self-reflection, sometimes students lack the language to articulate their thoughts about a particular subject. Teachers can provide scaffolding on Google Forms by using features such as Likert scales, multiple-choice questions, or sentence stems. They can also make checklists on Google Forms; for example, the checklist may ask students how they feel about the project, and they can check certain emotions.

Goal Setting and Progress Monitoring

People in many educational environments have negative views of the term *progress monitoring* because they usually associate it with standardized test scores. Often, progress monitoring ties into heavy-handed management and shame-based tactics for teachers whose students fall behind. However, teachers don't have to do it this way. The key to making sure that goal setting and progress monitoring help students reach a place of optimal performance is to keep the goal-setting process student centered. Teachers can shift toward student-centered goal setting in the following ways.

- **Let students decide on the relevant metrics:** Although we want goals to be SMART (strategic and specific, measurable, attainable, results oriented, and time bound; Conzemius & O'Neill, 2014), we also want them to use relevant metrics. During a goal-setting conference, students can choose what they want to accomplish and how they will measure their progress. So a student's goal might be, "By the end of this week, I will be able to look at three different graphs and determine the equation."

- **Allow for multiple methods of progress tracking:** A simple Google Form can track progress over time in a powerful way. However, students can also reflect on their progress through keeping a journal or a Google Doc that they have shared with the teacher.

- **Remember the qualitative side of goal setting:** Sometimes, the best approach is to simply say, "What are your goals for this activity?" at the start of class and to end class with, "Did you reach your goal? Why or why not?"

- **Don't connect the progress to any external rewards:** Goal setting should be internally driven and based on things that matter to students. A student who really wants to improve as a reader might set a goal like, "I want to read fluently at grade level by the end of the quarter," but the goal isn't tied to Accelerated Reader points or to certificates and badges. The reward is the internal satisfaction of accomplishing a difficult task.

Student-Teacher Conferencing

Teachers can help students get a sense of progress through frequent one-on-one conferences. Teachers can meet with students for five minutes at a time and engage in conversations that help them articulate their level of mastery.

The idea is simple. If you meet with students for five minutes apiece, you can meet with thirty students over the course of a week by holding six conferences a day. This gets trickier in middle school and high school, where a teacher might not have a full thirty minutes open per class period. However, most department teachers have fifteen minutes they can spare per class period when students are working independently or in groups.

In my experience, student-teacher conferences best happen when students work independently or in groups. I've found that the warm-up and collaborative times, where students work on their projects in groups, make great conferencing times. You should have the conversations at a time when students can afford to miss five minutes of work, when the rest of the class doesn't need much teacher support, and when the classroom noise level stays loud enough that students won't worry about classmates eavesdropping. I've also found that it helps to move away from the rest of the class a little bit at a standing center while keeping an eye on the class.

There are three types of student-teacher conferences: (1) advice conferences, (2) reflection conferences, and (3) assessment conferences.

Advice Conferences

An advice conference focuses on students learning specific skills that they don't yet have. Each student asks the teacher a series of questions based on an area where he or she struggles. This provides a chance for targeted, one-on-one attention and explicit help with a strategy. Students guide the process, tapping into the teacher's expertise. This conference encourages students to embrace the idea that mistakes are part of the learning process. It sets up a classroom culture where students must have enough humility to admit that they still struggle in some area of learning. This gives students a chance to get targeted feedback they can use to grow more self-aware and, in the process, set better goals (Spencer, 2015). Advice conferences also allow the teacher to see more intensive issues that might require targeted tutoring.

Advice conferences help promote the growth mindset in every student (Dweck, 2008). Instead of waiting for a teacher to say if something is right or wrong, students learn the art of asking for help. While this conference style allows students to ask specific questions and seek out specific teacher feedback, it does not make them helpless and dependent.

Sometimes, these conversations begin with examining student work. Here, students might come with a list of clarifying questions about specific skills they are trying to master. Other times, they might come with a concept that they still struggle with.

The following question stems can help students refine what they want to ask. Visit **go.SolutionTree.com/instruction** for a free reproducible version of these stems.

- "Could you show me how to _____?"

- "I'm going to practice _____; can you to tell me what you notice that I might be missing?"

- "I'm stuck on _____. What resources would you recommend for me?"

- "How could I improve on _____?"

- "I tried to do _____, but it isn't working. What am I missing?"

- "When I _____, I sometimes have a hard time with _____. How do I get past this?"

- "_____ still really confuses me because _____. How can I better understand this?"

Reflection Conferences

In a reflection conference, instead of telling students what to do, the teacher aims to draw out student reflection. The teacher uses a series of reflective questions to lead students through the metacognition process and into setting and monitoring goals. As the year progresses, the teacher asks fewer follow-up questions, and students begin sharing how they are doing without the aid of prechosen questions (Spencer, 2015).

The teacher should not correct students or give practical ideas in a reflection conference. Instead, the teacher asks reflective questions that encourage students to think about their learning.

The conference typically starts with the teacher reminding the student of the conference's purpose: reflection. Next, it moves toward a discussion about strengths and weaknesses. Here, the teacher shouldn't add any specific strengths or weaknesses; rather, he or she should simply aim to get the student thinking, reflecting, and sharing. It ends with an articulation of goals and a plan for next steps. So the general trajectory of the conversation moves from vague and personal to specific and practical.

In this conference, it is important to avoid feedback. Avoid talking about scores, grades, or rubrics students have filled out. Teachers may find this tricky at first. Sometimes, students fear saying the wrong thing and will ask, "Is that right?" They might hedge their self-reflection with phrases like, "I don't really know, but maybe . . ." However, the more they engage in reflection, the more they grow confident in their ability to self-reflect.

I ask students the following questions in this style of conference. Visit **go.Solution Tree.com/instruction** for a free reproducible version of these stems.

- "What are some strategies that you have mastered? Why do you feel you have mastered them?"

- "In what area do you still struggle?"

- "Describe your process when you _____. What happens in this process?"

- "What I'm hearing you say is _____. Is that accurate?"

- "In what areas are you growing? Are there any areas that you don't see growth in?"

- "How do you feel _____ is going? Is it turning out the way you planned?"

- "What are some things you notice about _____?"

- "In terms of _____, what will success look like?"

- "What do you hope to learn?"

Assessment Conferences

Unlike the reflection conference, the assessment conference focuses less on reflecting on the metacognition process and more on students judging their own content mastery. Using a standards-based assessment grid during an assessment conference is the basis for specific progress monitoring, and at the end, students set their own goals (Spencer, 2015). See figure 4.1.

The goals of an assessment conference are to examine student work (including rubrics and self-assessments) and have a conversation about standard mastery. While advice conferences involve students asking teachers questions, and reflection conferences involve the opposite, assessment conferences tend to have more of a give-and-take.

Prerequisite Skills

1. I can _____.

2. I can _____.

3. I can _____.

Level of Mastery

Objective	Level of Mastery	Student Feedback	Teacher Feedback
I can generate clarifying questions.	Meets the standards	I have an easy time making clarifying questions, but I sometimes don't know why I need to create these questions.	*Your clarifying questions are well crafted but you don't seem to seek out answers to the questions.*

Figure 4.1: Sample standards-based assessment grid.

Sometimes, it works best for teachers to start by asking students about what grade they feel they have earned and why. This leads to a deeper conversation about mastery and progress. Other times, it helps to start with an open gradebook and the question, "Do you feel this is accurate?" Still, often it works best to examine a project rubric that both the teacher and student filled out to compare and contrast perceptions. Ultimately, students should know which standards they have mastered and where they need to go next. Visit **go.SolutionTree.com/instruction** for the free reproducible "Standards-Based Assessment Grid Rubric."

You can ask students the following questions in assessment conferences.

- "How do you feel you have done on this standard? What level of mastery would you give yourself? Why?"

- "Does this accurately represent what you have learned?"

- "Which standards do you need to focus on in order to improve? What help do you need? Where will you look for that help?"

- "Which standards do you excel at? What kind of enrichment would you like to pursue in those areas?"

- "How will you know when you have mastered _____?"

- "What next steps do you need to take in order to master _____?"

See table 4.2 for a summary of the three types of conferences.

Table 4.2: Three Types of Conferences

	Advice Conference	Reflection Conference	Assessment Conference
Focus	The teacher gives students targeted help and instruction in specific areas.	The teacher guides students toward self-reflection.	The teacher has a conversation about standard mastery.
Student's Role	The student asks questions and seeks out specific feedback.	The student answers questions and reflects on learning.	The student talks about progress toward specific standards.
Teacher's Role	The teacher answers questions with accuracy and precision and allows the student to practice a strategy under supervision.	The teacher asks questions, paraphrases answers, and guides the student toward self-reflection.	The teacher asks questions about progress and shares information based on evidence of student work.
Further Application	The student leaves with actionable steps to fix particular work.	The student can plan for and select strategies for future improvement based on self-reflection.	The student can figure out what standards he or she still needs to master and how to get there.
Role in Cultivating a Growth Mindset	Every student has a chance to admit failure and learn from it.	Every student has a chance to articulate areas where he or she needs to grow.	Every student realizes that he or she gets as many retakes as necessary until mastery.

Source: Spencer, 2015.

Horizontal assessment empowers students to set goals and monitor their own progress through self-, peer-, and teacher-led assessment. As a result, students can determine what they know, what they don't know, and what they need to do in order to reach their goals. This sense of progression helps lead students toward a state of flow.

Action Steps

The following action steps can help you shift from top-down to horizontal assessment.

- **Give students time to self-reflect:** Build it into your lesson plans.

- **Implement a student-teacher conferencing system:** If you devote five minutes per week with each student, your students will have a better sense of their own progress toward mastering standards.

- **Have students create their own goals and track their progress toward mastery:** However, this doesn't have to entail a written task with charts and graphs. Students can think about their goals without stopping their work.

- **Structure activities with an embedded sense of progress:** Students need to know exactly where they are and what they need to do to move on. Find ways to make progress visible for students.

Epilogue

We know what it feels like to reach a state of flow. It often includes almost paradoxical extremes simultaneously. You hyperfocus on what you are doing, completely aware of your surroundings, while also tuning things out. You constantly monitor your performance and adjust based on feedback, yet you feel as if you aren't thinking. Action and awareness have a deep connection, but flow can feel almost otherworldly. Time seems to speed up and slow down.

We know what flow looks like for our students. We see it on both an individual and group level. It feels almost magical when students get collectively lost in reading a novel, writing a blog post, solving a problem, or prototyping a product. These moments fuel our passion and give us a vision for what student engagement can look like.

It's easy, then, to view flow as something mysterious. However, I have written this book to demystify flow and explore practical structures we can set up in our classrooms to make it happen. It begins with shifting to intrinsic motivation and moving instruction toward personalization. It involves a different classroom pace, free of disruptions and interruptions. It requires a balance of challenge and skill for all students. Students need to see the constant progression toward their goals through immediate, meaningful feedback.

Final Thoughts

Flow is not a program. It's not a step-by-step recipe for fixing student engagement. Instead, it acts as a lens for making sense of what it means to reach the next level of student engagement. It's a different way of thinking about student engagement, where students go beyond compliance and toward empowerment.

We want classrooms to become spaces of optimal engagement. We know that students need this, not because it leads to higher achievement or better test scores but because it's part of what makes life awesome. Yes, sometimes I try to justify student engagement as a means to an end, as engaged students often learn more. And engaged students often score higher on tests. However, one of the takeaways of flow theory is that this state of optimal engagement is an end in itself. In these moments, you feel the most alive. In these moments, you experience joy and contentment. These moments make life enjoyable. Don't we want that for our students?

References and Resources

Anderson, L. W., & Krathwohl, D. R. (Eds.). (2001). *A taxonomy for learning, teaching, and assessing: A revision of Bloom's taxonomy of educational objectives*. Boston: Allyn & Bacon.

Azzam, A. M. (2007). Special report: Why students drop out. *Educational Leadership, 64*(7), 91–93. Accessed at www.ascd.org/publications /educational-leadership/apr07/vol64/num07/Why-Students-Drop-Out .aspx on January 3, 2015.

Balu, R., Zhu, P., Doolittle, F., Schiller, E., Jenkins, J., & Gersten, R. (2015). *Evaluation of response to intervention practices for elementary school reading* (Report No. NCEE 2016–4000). Washington, DC: U.S. Department of Education, National Center for Education Evaluation and Regional Assistance, Institute of Education Sciences. Accessed at http://ies .ed.gov/ncee/pubs/20164000/pdf/20164000.pdf on June 27, 2016.

Bandura, A. (Ed.). (1995). *Self-efficacy in changing societies*. New York: Cambridge University Press.

Buffum, A., Mattos, M., & Weber, C. (2009). *Pyramid response to intervention: RTI, professional learning communities, and how to respond when kids don't learn*. Bloomington, IN: Solution Tree Press.

Busteed, B. (2013, January 7). *The school cliff: Student engagement drops with each school year* [Blog post]. Accessed at www.gallup.com/opinion/gallup /170525/school-cliff-student-engagement-drops-school-year.aspx on October 10, 2014.

Conzemius, A. E., & O'Neill, J. (2014). *The handbook for SMART school teams: Revitalizing best practices for collaboration* (2nd ed.). Bloomington, IN: Solution Tree Press.

Cordova, D. I., & Lepper, M. R. (1996). Intrinsic motivation and the process of learning: Beneficial effects of contextualization, personalization, and choice. *Journal of Educational Psychology, 88*(4), 715–730.

Csikszentmihalyi, M. (1990). *Flow: The psychology of optimal experience.* New York: Harper & Row.

Csikszentmihalyi, M. (2002). *Mihaly Csikszentmihalyi: Motivating people to learn.* Accessed at www.edutopia.org/mihaly-csikszentmihalyi -motivating-people-learn on October 9, 2016.

Deci, E. L. (1971). Effects of externally mediated rewards on intrinsic motivation. *Journal of Personality and Social Psychology, 18*(1), 105–115.

Deci, E. L. (1995). *Why we do what we do: Understanding self-motivation.* New York: Penguin Books.

D'Onfro, J. (2015, April 17). The truth about Google's famous "20% time" policy. *Business Insider.* Accessed at www.businessinsider.com/google-20 -percent-time-policy-2015-4 on September 28, 2016.

Dweck, C. S. (2008). *Mindset: The new psychology of success.* New York: Ballantine Books.

Elias, M. J. (2016, January 14). *How and why intrinsic motivation works* [Blog post]. Accessed at www.edutopia.org/blog/how-and-why-intrinsic -motivation-works-maurice-elias on October 9, 2016.

Fisher, A. V., Godwin, K. E., & Seltman, H. (2014). Visual environment, attention allocation, and learning in young children: When too much of a good thing may be bad. *Psychological Science, 25*(7), 1362–1370.

Gallagher, K. (2009). *Readicide: How schools are killing reading and what you can do about it.* Portland, ME: Stenhouse.

Gallagher, K. (2010). Reversing readicide. *Educational Leadership, 67*(6), 36–41. Accessed at www.ascd.org/publications/educational-leadership /mar10/vol67/num06/Reversing-Readicide.aspx on September 30, 2016.

Ginsburg, D. (2013, December 1). *My biggest regret as a teacher: Extrinsic rewards* [Blog post]. Accessed at http://blogs.edweek.org/teachers/coach _gs_teaching_tips/2013/12/my_biggest_regret_as_a_teacher_extrinsic _rewards.html on September 28, 2016.

Hart, B. A., Gilner, F. H., Handal, P. J., & Gfeller, J. D. (1998). The relationship between perfectionism and self-efficacy. *Personality and Individual Differences, 24*(1), 109–113.

Hendron, J. (2014, May 12). *How engaged is engaged?* [Blog post]. Accessed at http://blogs.glnd.k12.va.us/jhendron/2014/05/12/how-engaged-is -engaged on June 27, 2016.

Hom, E. J. (2014, February 11). What is STEM education? *Live Science.* Accessed at www.livescience.com/43296-what-is-stem-education.html on July 20, 2016.

Jennings, P. A. (2015). *Mindfulness for teachers: Simple skills for peace and productivity in the classroom.* New York: Norton.

Juliani, A. J. (2013, June 25). *Why "20% time" is good for schools* [Blog post]. Accessed at www.edutopia.org/blog/20-percent-time-a-j-juliani on September 28, 2016.

Juliani, A. J. (2016). *The 10 most asked questions about Genius Hour and 20% time projects.* Accessed at http://ajjuliani.com/the-10-most-asked -questions-about-genius-hour-and-20-time-projects on September 10, 2016.

Kohn, A. (1993). *Punished by rewards: The trouble with gold stars, incentive plans, A's, praise, and other bribes.* Boston: Houghton Mifflin.

Massimini, F., Csikszentmihalyi, M., & Carli, M. (1987). The monitoring of optimal experience: A tool for psychiatric rehabilitation. *Journal of Nervous and Mental Disease, 175*(9), 545–549.

McLeod, S. (2014, December 22). We need schools to be different. *The Huffington Post.* Accessed at www.huffingtonpost.com/scott-mcleod/we -need-schools-to-be-dif_b_6353198.html on June 28, 2016.

McLeod, S. (2016, March 16). *The biggest indictment of our schools is not their failure to raise test scores* [Blog post]. Accessed at http://dangerously irrelevant.org/2016/03/the-biggest-indictment-of-our-schools-is-not -their-failure-to-raise-test-scores.html on June 27, 2016.

Muller, D. A. (2008). *Designing effective multimedia for physics education: A thesis submitted in fulfillment of the requirements for the degree of doctor of philosophy* (Doctoral thesis). Accessed at http://sydney.edu.au/science /physics/pdfs/research/super/PhD(Muller).pdf on July 19, 2016.

Nakamura, J., & Csikszentmihalyi, C. (2009). Flow theory and research. In C. R. Snyder & S. J. Lopez (Eds.), *The Oxford handbook of positive psychology* (2nd ed., pp. 195–206). Oxford, NY: Oxford University Press.

National Governors Association Center for Best Practices & Council of Chief State School Officers. (2010). *Common Core State Standards for English language arts and literacy in history/social studies, science, and technical subjects.* Washington DC: Author Accessed at www.corestandards.org /ELA-Literacy on October 9, 2016.

Newport, C. (2016). *Deep work: Rules for focused success in a distracted world.* New York: Grand Central.

Paul, A. M. (2013, February 19). How to use deliberate confusion to learn faster. *Business Insider.* Accessed at www.businessinsider.com/confusion-is -actually-a-good-thing-2013-2 on September 30, 2016.

Pink, D. H. (2009). *Drive: The surprising truth about what motivates us.* New York: Riverhead Books.

Ripp, P. (2014, September 6). *Before you assign a reading log* [Blog post]. Accessed at https://pernillesripp.com/2014/09/06/before-you-assign-a -reading-log on September 28, 2016.

Rose, J. (2012, May 9). How to break free of our 19th-century factory-model education system. *The Atlantic.* Accessed at www.theatlantic.com /business/archive/2012/05/how-to-break-free-of-our-19th-century -factory-model-education-system/256881 on September 30, 2016.

Schaffer, O. (2013). *Crafting fun user experiences: A method to facilitate flow* [White paper]. Accessed at www.humanfactors.com/whitepapers/crafting _fun_ux.asp on June 27, 2016.

Schlechty, P. C. (2011). *Engaging students: The next level of working on the work.* San Francisco: Jossey-Bass.

Smith, K. S., Rook, J. E., & Smith, T. W. (2007). Increasing student engagement using effective and metacognitive writing strategies in content areas. *Preventing School Failure: Alternative Education for Children and Youth, 51*(3), 43–48.

Spencer, J. (2015, April 9). *The power of student conferencing* [Blog post]. Accessed at www.spencerauthor.com/2015/04/the-power-of-student -conferencing.html on August 11, 2016.

Stanney, K. M., & Hale, K. S. (2012). (Eds.). *Advances in cognitive engineering and neuroergonomics*. Boca Raton, FL: CRC Press.

Suttie, J. (2012, April 16). Can schools help students find flow? *Greater Good*. Accessed at http://greatergood.berkeley.edu/article/item/can_schools_help _students_find_flow on September 30, 2016.

Svinicki, M. D. (2016). *Motivation: An updated analysis. Motivation: An updated analysis—IDEA paper 59* [White paper]. Accessed at http://idea edu.org/wp-content/uploads/2016/05/PaperIDEA_59.pdf on October 9, 2016.

West-Puckett, S. (2013, September 13). *ReMaking education: Designing classroom makerspaces for transformative learning* [Blog post]. Accessed at www.edutopia.org/blog/classroom-makerspaces-transformative-learning -stephanie-west-puckett on July 20, 2016.

Solutions for Creating the Learning Spaces Students Deserve

Solutions Series: Solutions for Creating the Learning Spaces Students Deserve reimagines the norms defining K–12 education. In a short, reader-friendly format, these books challenge traditional thinking about schooling and encourage readers to question their beliefs about what real teaching and learning look like in action.

Creating a Culture of Feedback
William M. Ferriter and Paul J. Cancellieri
BKF731

Embracing a Culture of Joy
Dean Shareski
BKF730

Making Learning Flow
John Spencer
BKF733

Reimagining Literacy Through Global Collaboration
Pernille Ripp
BKF732

Wait! Your professional development journey doesn't have to end with the last pages of this book.

We realize improving student learning doesn't happen overnight. And your school or district shouldn't be left to puzzle out all the details of this process alone.

No matter where you are on the journey, we're committed to helping you get to the next stage.

Take advantage of everything from **custom workshops** to **keynote presentations** and **interactive web and video conferencing**. We can even help you develop an action plan tailored to fit your specific needs.

Let's get the conversation started.

Call 888.763.9045 today.

SolutionTree.com